I0818563

EVERYTHING X SPORTS
EVERYTHING
NBA
BY RACHEL GRACK
eureka!

Eureka! books turn real stories into unforgettable experiences. This nonfiction imprint sparks curiosity, encourages critical thinking, and engages middle-grade readers. *Eureka!* books empower young minds to explore the stories of the real world, one fascinating fact at a time. Unravel the power of knowledge and lifelong learning with *Eureka!*

This edition first published in 2026 by Bellwether Media, Inc.

Library of Congress Cataloging-in-Publication Data

Names: Grack, Rachel, 1973- author.
Title: Everything NBA / By Rachel Grack.
Description: Eureka!. | Minnetonka, MN : Bellwether Media, Inc., 2026. | Series: Everything sports | Includes index. | Audience: Ages 9-15 | Audience: Grades 7-9 | Summary: "Engaging images accompany information on NBA. The text level and subject matter are intended for students in grades 5 through 9"-- Provided by publisher.
Identifiers: LCCN 2025020011 (print) | LCCN 2025020012 (ebook) | ISBN 9798893045598 (library binding) | ISBN 9798893046977 (ebook)
Subjects: LCSH: National Basketball Association--History--Juvenile literature.
Classification: LCC GV885.515.N37 G598 2026 (print) | LCC GV885.515.N37 (ebook) | DDC 796.323/640973--dc23/eng/20250520
LC record available at https://lccn.loc.gov/2025020011
LC ebook record available at https://lccn.loc.gov/2025020012

Editor: Kieran Downs Designer: Jeffrey Kollock

Printed in the United States of America, North Mankato, MN.

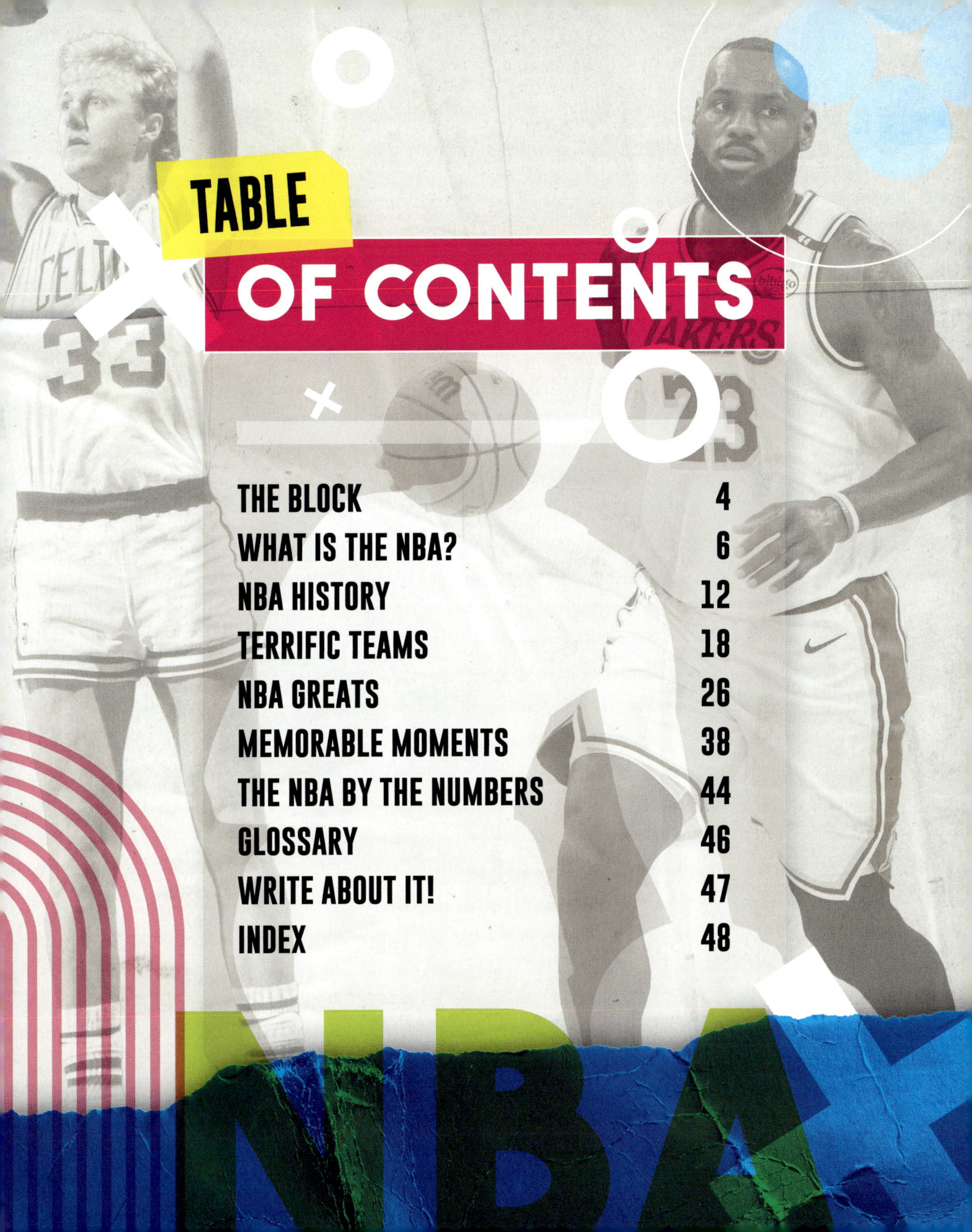

TABLE OF CONTENTS

THE BLOCK

It is the closing minutes of Game 7 of the 2016 NBA Finals. LeBron James and the Cleveland Cavaliers are battling the Golden State Warriors. The Cavaliers have fought their way to Game 7. After losing three of the first four games, the Cavaliers won two in a row to force Game 7.

After trailing at halftime, the Cavaliers have battled back to tie the game 89–89. Then, neither team scores for minutes as they engage in an intense defensive battle. With 1:56 on the clock, Warriors player Andre Iguodala grabs a defensive rebound and makes a **fast break**. He fires a pass to teammate Stephen Curry, who quickly bounces the ball back to him. Iguodala looks sure to score as he goes for the layup. But he is chased down by LeBron James! Out of nowhere, James blocks the shot from behind! Minutes later, Cavaliers player Kyrie Irving hits a 3-pointer, and the Cavaliers win the game.

James's block helped the Cavaliers win their first-ever NBA championship. They are the first team in history to win the Finals after trailing a series 3–1.

THE BLOCK

TOP SPEED

LeBron James ran 20.1 miles (32.3 kilometers) per hour during the block. He jumped 35 inches (89 centimeters) into the air.

CURRY
30
LOVE
0
The Finals
GOLDEN STATE
30
WARRIORS
NBA CHAMPS
2016
NBA TV

WHAT IS THE NBA?

The National Basketball Association (NBA) is a professional men's basketball league. It is made up of 29 teams from the United States and one team from Canada. Each team's **roster** can carry a maximum of 15 players. The NBA has **headquarters** in New York and New Jersey. But the league features the best players from around the world. The 2024–25 rosters included 125 international players from 43 countries and territories. Games are broadcast all over the world.

NBA teams are split between the Western **Conference** and the Eastern Conference. Each 15-team conference has three **divisions** with five teams each. The Western Conference consists of the Northwest, Pacific, and Southwest Divisions. The Eastern Conference breaks into the Atlantic, Central, and Southeast Divisions.

NBA HEADQUARTERS, NEW YORK

NBA DIVISIONS

WESTERN CONFERENCE

Northwest Division

Pacific Division

Southwest Division

EASTERN CONFERENCE

Atlantic Division

Central Division

Southeast Division

The six NBA divisions were introduced before the 2004–05 season. Teams do not have to win their divisions in order to make the **playoffs**. Instead, they are used to determine game schedules. The divisions have created heated rivalries that get fans fired up. These teams have faced off in some unforgettable games.

The NBA regular season runs from October through April. Each team plays 82 games. They play three or four games against opponents in their conference. Teams play other teams within their divisions four times. They play twice at home and twice on the road. Teams also face teams in the opposing conference twice a year. They play once at home and once away. Eight teams from each conference make the playoffs. The top six teams with the best win-loss records are guaranteed a spot. The other two teams are determined by the NBA Play-In **Tournament**.

The Play-In Tournament immediately follows the regular season. Teams in seventh to tenth place battle for the final two playoff **seeds**. In each conference, the seventh-place team plays the eighth-place team. The winner of the matchup secures the seventh seed. But the loser still has a chance to clinch the eighth seed. The teams in ninth and tenth place also face each other. The loser of this matchup is eliminated. The winner plays the loser of the seven-versus-eight game. This game determines the eighth seed.

PLAY-IN TOURNAMENT

ROOKIE OF THE YEAR

Award given to the top rookie of the regular season

DEFENSIVE PLAYER OF THE YEAR

Award given to the best defensive player of the regular season

PLAYOFF GAME

Once seeds are set, four rounds of playoffs begin. Matchups are decided by seed. In the first round, the first seed plays the eighth seed, the second seed faces the seventh seed, the third seed matches up with the sixth seed, and the fourth seed plays the fifth seed. Each round has teams play a best-of-seven series. The first two games are played at the higher seed's home court. The next two games are played at the lower seed's court. Games then go back-and-forth between courts until one team wins four games. The winner of each series moves on to the next round. The last teams standing in each conference square off in the NBA Finals. The winner is the NBA champion!

NBA FINALS

The NBA **Draft** takes place each year in June. It offers teams the chance to add new players who have not played in the NBA before. Draft picks can be college athletes or professional players from other leagues around the world. They must be at least 19 years old and out of high school for one year. The 14 lowest-ranking teams get the top picks assigned through the NBA Draft Lottery. Then, the remaining 16 teams pick in order according to their **standings**. The draft consists of two rounds, during which a total of 60 players are drafted.

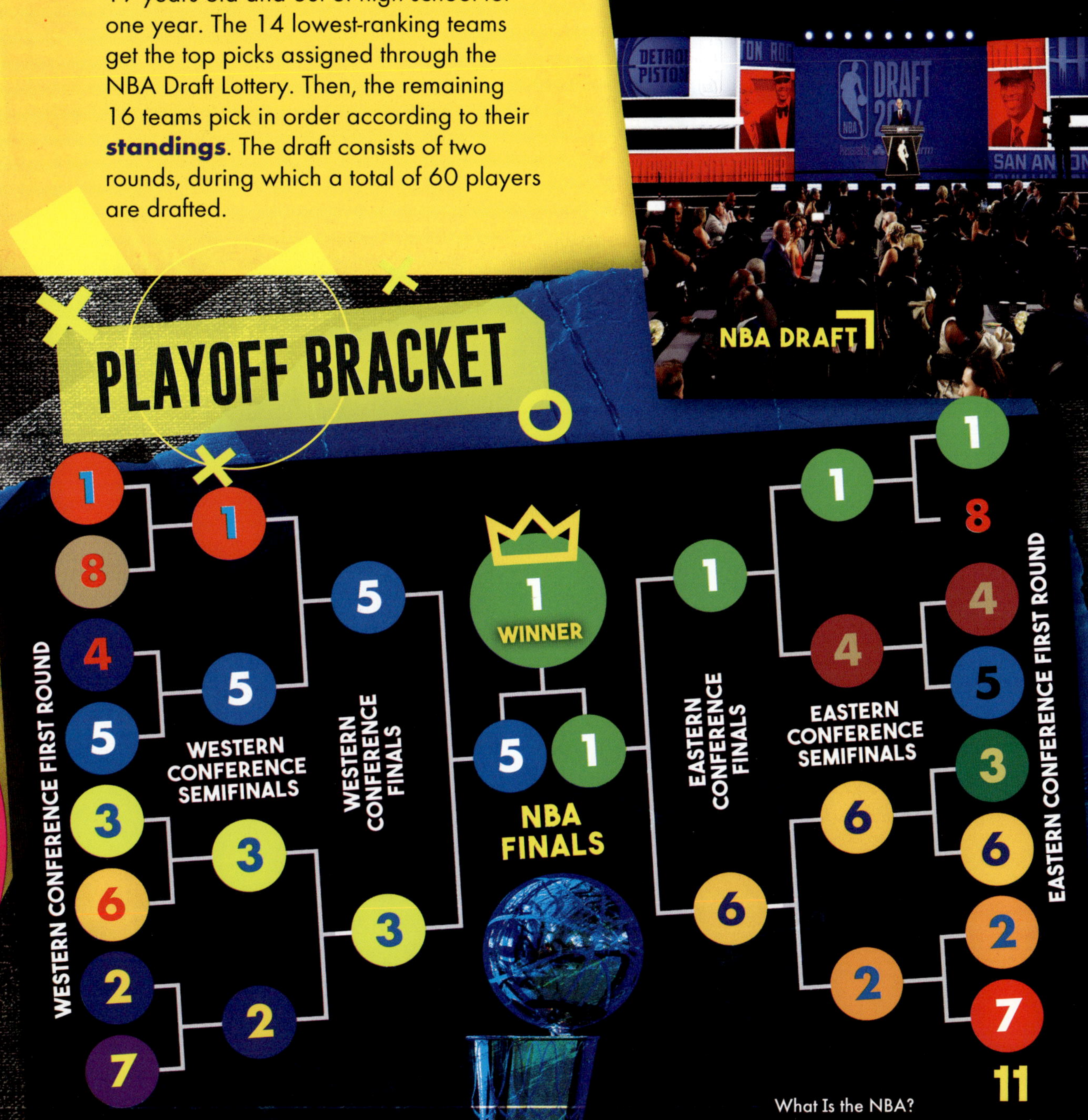

NBA HISTORY

Professional basketball began in 1898 with the National Basketball League (NBL). But it was poorly organized and disbanded in 1904. In 1935, the league restructured with a group of teams mostly across the Upper Midwest. In 1946, the Basketball Association of America (BAA) formed as the NBL's rival league. It gained a large following by establishing teams in bigger cities and holding games in large arenas. By 1948, the BAA had attracted many of the NBL's top players, as well as four of its **franchises**. The two leagues decided to **merge** rather than compete. On August 3, 1949, they formed the National Basketball Association (NBA).

At the beginning, the NBA struggled. The league started out with 17 teams. But fan support dwindled. By 1954, the number of teams dropped to eight. Hoping to make games more exciting, the league added new rules such as the **shot clock**. This created much faster gameplay with a significant increase in scoring. The league also made changes to how many free throws teams were rewarded after fouls. This helped reduce the number of fouls and increased scoring. These changes helped the league gain many fans.

BAA GAME, 1949

FIRST SHOT CLOCK

NBL AND BAA MERGER

Between 1957 and 1969, the Boston Celtics helped establish the NBA's popularity. They were the top team in the league for over a decade, winning 11 championships in 13 seasons. The Celtics also inspired social change in the NBA. In 1964, they became the first team in the league to play an all-Black starting lineup. Star players such as Wilt Chamberlain, Oscar Robertson, and Bill Russell also helped the league gain fans.

BOSTON CELTICS, 1967

ABA GAME, 1971

In 1967, a new league of 11 teams formed the American Basketball Association (ABA). This league rivaled the NBA. Each season, the ABA and NBA battled to lure the top college players. In 1968, the NBA added two teams. Three more teams joined in 1970. By 1974, the NBA was up to 18 teams. In 1976, the ABA **dissolved**, and four of its teams moved to the NBA.

In 1979, the NBA added the 3-point shot popularized in the ABA. This change created even more scoring. Expansion continued into the 1980s with five more teams joining the league, bringing the league up to 27 teams. Extraordinary players such as Larry Bird and Magic Johnson boosted the NBA's popularity during this time. The heated rivalry between Johnson's Los Angeles Lakers and Bird's Celtics drew large crowds and fueled record TV ratings.

3-POINT SHOT

LARRY BIRD AND MAGIC JOHNSON, 1985

DAVID STERN WITH MICHAEL JORDAN

BASKETBALL AFRICA LEAGUE GAME

In 1984, David Stern took over as **commissioner**. He reshaped the NBA into a worldwide entertainment industry. Stern set limits on how much a team could spend on player salaries. This prevented wealthy franchises from hoarding talent and kept competition fair. He also negotiated broadcasting deals with major television networks to help the league reach even more people. Stern also promoted star players through aggressive marketing. The biggest star he promoted was Michael Jordan, who joined the Chicago Bulls in 1984. His dazzling on-court performance made him an off-court celebrity. Jordan and the Bulls ruled the 1990s, winning six championships in eight years.

The early 2000s featured superstars like LeBron James and Shaquille O'Neal. The Charlotte Bobcats became the league's 30th team in 2004. The 2010s starred players such as Stephen Curry, Kevin Durant, and James Harden. In 2016, the league opened its Global Academy in Canberra, Australia. This training center works to develop talented young players from around the world. In 2019, the NBA launched the Basketball Africa League (BAL). The BAL features 12 teams with players from many different African countries. Today, the NBA is a premier sports organization. Each generation of players pushes professional basketball to new heights.

TIMELINE

1935

The NBL forms

1946

The BAA forms as a rival to the NBL

1949

The NBL and the BAA merge into the NBA

1954

New rules help the league gain fans

1967

The ABA forms

1976

The ABA dissolves and four of its teams join the NBA

1979

Larry Bird and Magic Johnson join the NBA

1984

David Stern becomes the NBA commissioner and transforms league

2016

NBA Global Academy opens

2019

Basketball Africa League forms

TERRIFIC TEAMS

1985–86 BOSTON CELTICS

The 1985–86 Boston Celtics teamed up five future Hall of Famers. The starting lineup included Larry Bird and Kevin McHale as forwards and Robert Parish at center. This trio became known as the "Big Three." To fill out the starting lineup, Dennis Johnson played point guard, and Danny Ainge played shooting guard. Sixth Man of the Year winner Bill Walton helped the team as a key **bench player**. The Celtics finished the regular season with the best record in the league. They lost only one game on their home court.

Their first playoff matchup was against the Chicago Bulls. They **swept** the series. Next, the Celtics faced the Atlanta Hawks. The Celtics won the series in five games. They dominated the Milwaukee Bucks in Eastern Conference Finals to qualify for their third Finals in a row.

In the Finals, the Celtics squared off with the Houston Rockets. The Celtics took the first two wins in Boston. In Houston, the Rockets won a close Game 3, but fell to the Celtics by 3 points in Game 4. In Game 5, the Rockets snatched another victory. Game 6 was played in Boston. The Celtics dominated the Rockets 114–97, winning their record 16th championship.

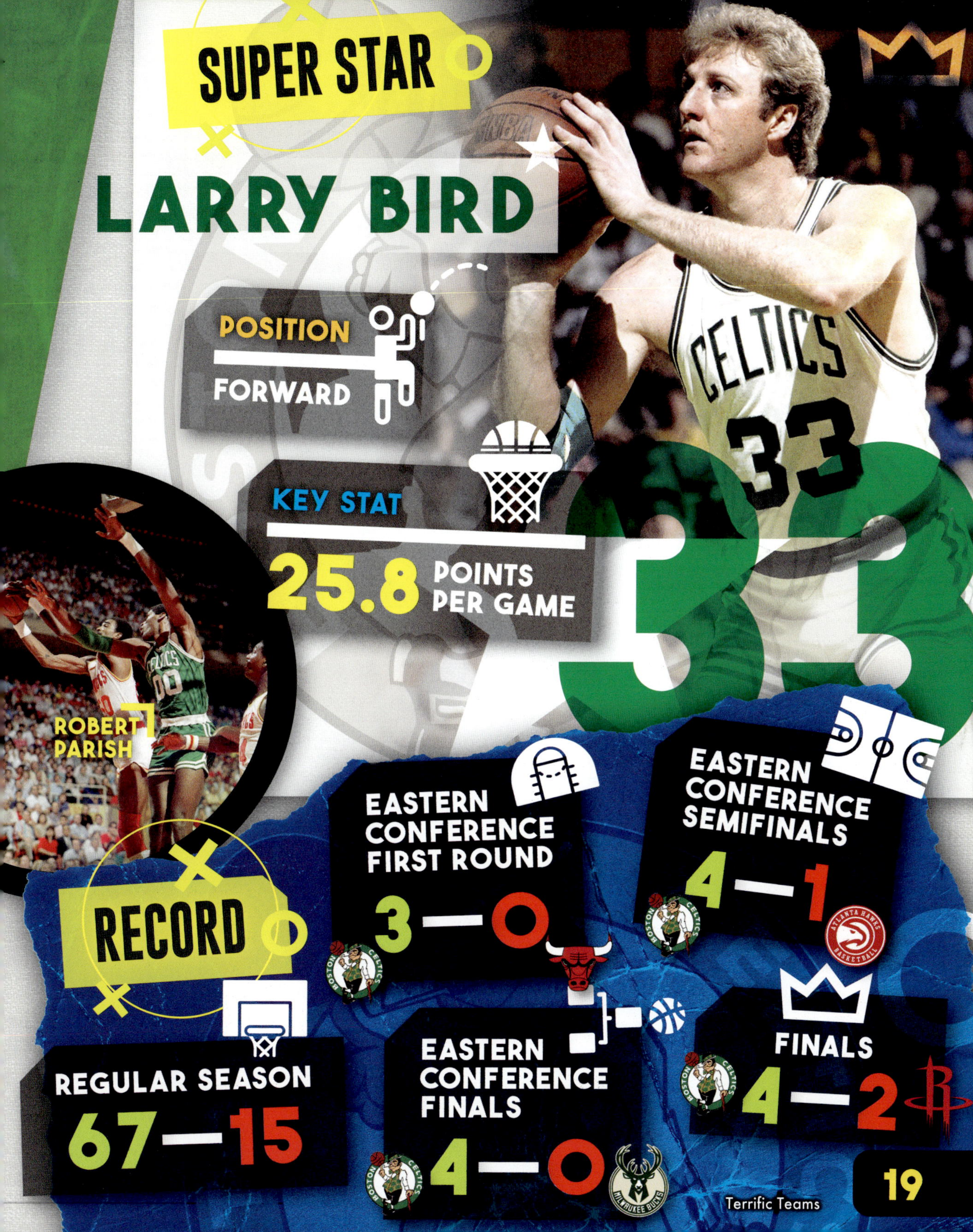
SUPER STAR
LARRY BIRD
POSITION
FORWARD
KEY STAT
25.8 POINTS PER GAME
33
ROBERT PARISH
RECORD
REGULAR SEASON
67—15
EASTERN CONFERENCE FIRST ROUND
3—0
EASTERN CONFERENCE SEMIFINALS
4—1
EASTERN CONFERENCE FINALS
4—0
FINALS
4—2

1995–96 CHICAGO BULLS

Led by the NBA's 1995–96 Most Valuable Player (MVP) Michael Jordan, the 1995–96 Chicago Bulls shattered league records and created new ones. The starting lineup also included future Hall of Famers Scottie Pippen and Dennis Rodman. Point guard Steve Kerr and forward Toni Kukoč were important bench players. This star-studded team was led by future Hall of Fame Coach Phil Jackson.

Coach Jackson ran a Triangle Offense. Players formed a triangle shape on the court and moved the ball between each other. This helped the Bulls lead the league in scoring. They were the first team in history to win over 70 games in a regular season. This record included an 18-game winning streak.

In the first round of the playoffs the Bulls swept the Miami Heat. Next, they defeated the New York Knicks 4–1. In the Eastern Conference Finals, they swept the Orlando Magic. In the Finals, they faced off with the Seattle SuperSonics. The Bulls took the first three games. But the SuperSonics rallied two wins in a row to take the series back to Chicago's United Center for Game 6. The Bulls' home-court advantage proved unbeatable. They won 87–75, clinching their fourth NBA championship in six seasons.

SCOTTIE PIPPEN

DENNIS RODMAN

SUPER STAR

MICHAEL JORDAN

POSITION

SHOOTING GUARD

KEY STAT

30.4 POINTS PER GAME

RECORD

REGULAR SEASON

72—10

EASTERN CONFERENCE FIRST ROUND

3—0

EASTERN CONFERENCE SEMIFINALS

4—1

EASTERN CONFERENCE FINALS

4—0

FINALS

2000–01 LOS ANGELES LAKERS

DEREK FISHER

The Los Angeles Lakers entered the 2000–01 season as defending NBA champs. The team's lineup included All-Star shooting guard Kobe Bryant and the previous season's MVP, center Shaquille O'Neal. During the off-season, the Lakers upgraded their defense by signing power forward Horace Grant.

The Lakers faced some hardships at the beginning of the season. Point guard Derek Fisher missed the first 62 games with a broken foot. Star players O'Neal and Bryant did not get along with each other off of the court. At the **All-Star Break**, the team had already lost more games than the entire previous season. Games turned around when Fisher returned. The team finished the regular season with an eight-game winning streak and carried this momentum into the playoffs.

In the playoffs, the Lakers made history. They went undefeated in the first three rounds, including sweeping the top-seeded San Antonio Spurs in the Western Conference Finals. This sent them to the NBA Finals.

In the NBA Finals, they dueled the Philadelphia 76ers. The Lakers' winning streak ended in an overtime Game 1 loss. But they swept the next four games to win their second **consecutive** championship. The Lakers' 15–1 **postseason** record was the best in NBA history. This record would stand until 2017.

KOBE BRYANT

RECORD
REGULAR SEASON
56—26
WESTERN CONFERENCE FIRST ROUND
3—0
LOS ANGELES LAKERS
PORTLAND TRAIL BLAZERS
WESTERN CONFERENCE SEMIFINALS
LOS ANGELES LAKERS
4—0
SACRAMENTO KINGS
WESTERN CONFERENCE FINALS
4—0
LOS ANGELES LAKERS
SAN ANTONIO SPURS
FINALS
LOS ANGELES LAKERS
4—1
PHILADELPHIA 76ers
SUPER STAR
SHAQUILLE O'NEAL
POSITION
CENTER
KEY STAT
28.7 POINTS PER GAME
34

2016–17 GOLDEN STATE WARRIORS

The 2016–17 Golden State Warriors featured many star players. The lineup included Klay Thompson, Draymond Green, and the 2015–16 MVP Stephen Curry. During the off-season, they signed four-time NBA scoring champion Kevin Durant as a **free agent**. With Durant, the new roster formed the "Fantastic Four."

The Warriors broke over 20 NBA records to earn a 67–15 record. They were the first team to have four players hit four 3-point shots in one game. Thompson became the first player to score 60 points in under 30 minutes of gameplay. Green won Defensive Player of the Year after leading the league in steals. This dominance continued into the playoffs, where the Warriors swept opponents in the first three rounds. This included a win in Game 1 of the Western Conference Finals after trailing the San Antonio Spurs by 25 points.

In the Finals, they faced the Cleveland Cavaliers. The Warriors won the first three games to set a record 15-game playoff winning streak. They fell to the Cavaliers in Game 4. But they bounced back in Game 5 with a 129–120 victory to win their fifth NBA championship. Their 16–1 playoff record is the best in NBA history.

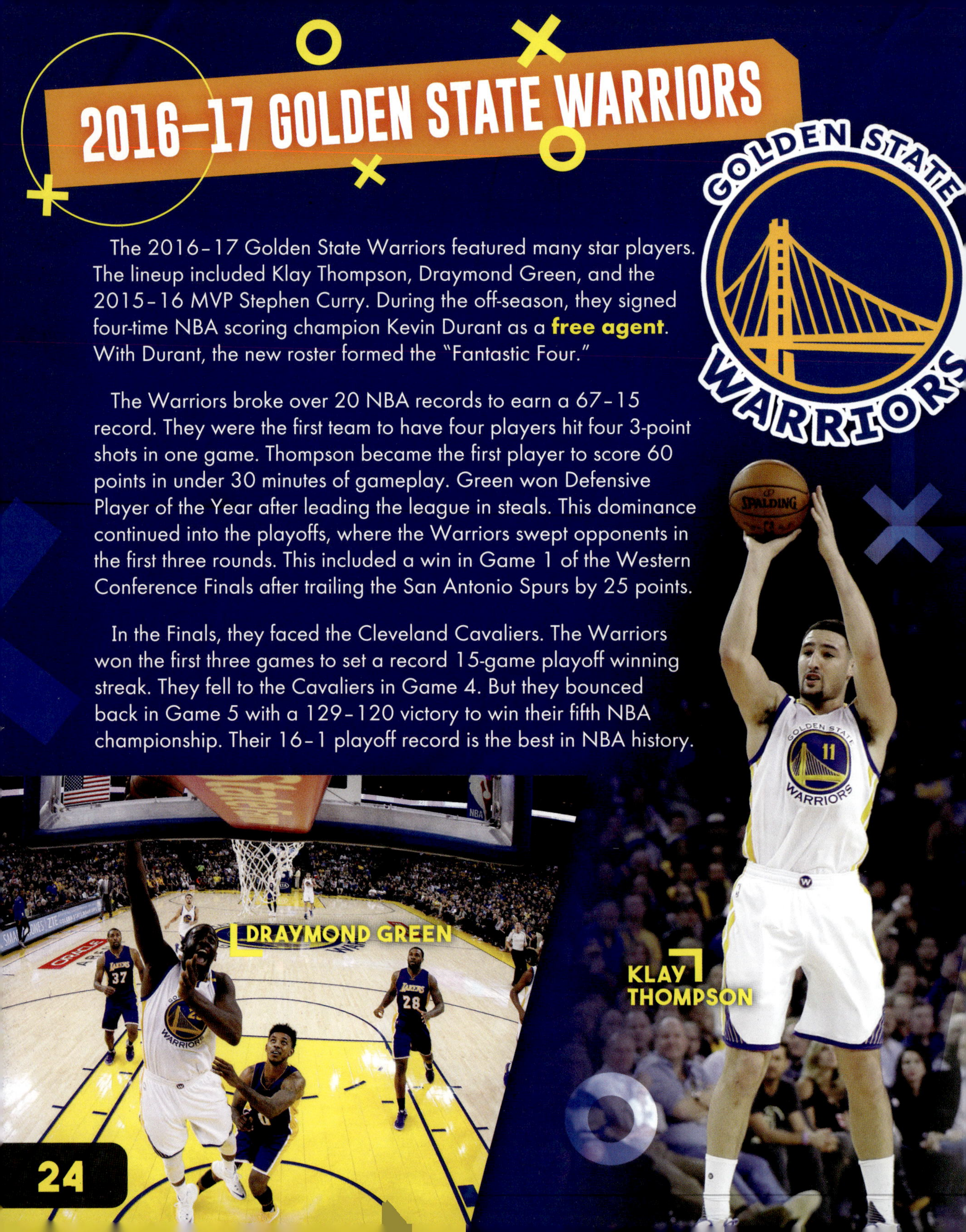

DRAYMOND GREEN

KLAY THOMPSON

SUPER STAR

KEVIN DURANT

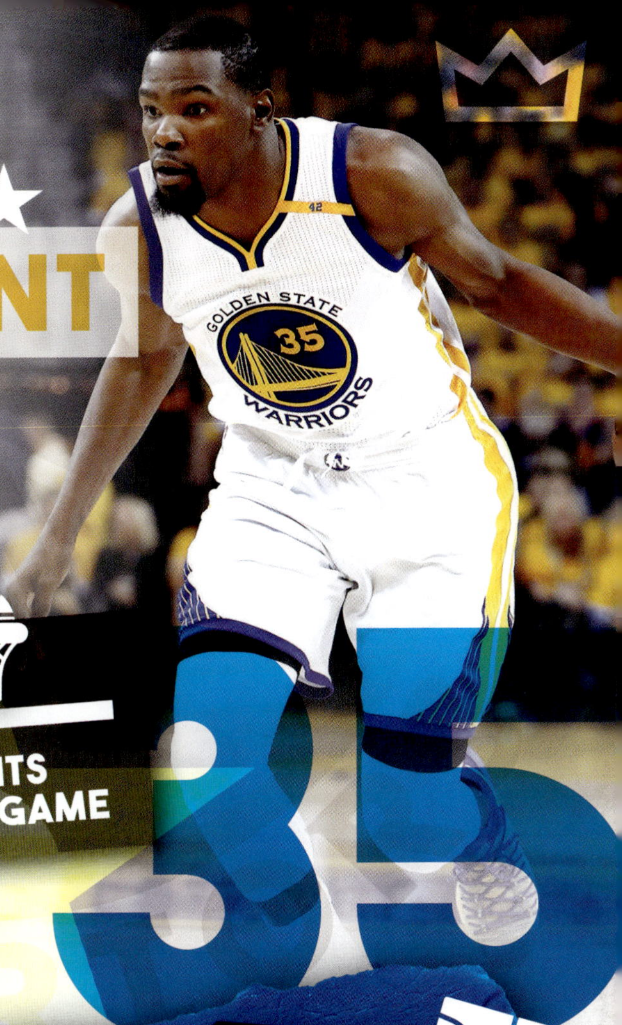

POSITION

POWER FORWARD

KEY STAT

25.1 POINTS PER GAME

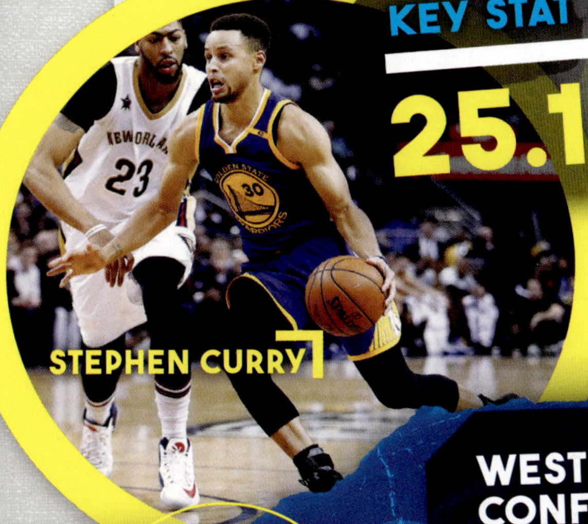

STEPHEN CURRY

RECORD

REGULAR SEASON

67—15

WESTERN CONFERENCE FIRST ROUND

4—0

WESTERN CONFERENCE SEMIFINALS

4—0

WESTERN CONFERENCE FINALS

4—0

FINALS

4—1

NBA GREATS

WILT CHAMBERLAIN

PLAYER #13

THE HARLEM GLOBETROTTERS

In the 1958–59 season, Chamberlain played for the Harlem Globetrotters. The Globetrotters are a show team. They perform tricks and comedic acts for audiences. The team still performs today!

Wilt Chamberlain was one of the highest-scoring basketball players of all time. Chamberlain joined the Philadelphia Warriors in 1959. In his first game, he scored 43 points. In his first season, he was named **Rookie** of the Year as well as league MVP.

Chamberlain's most famous season was 1961–62. That March, he became the first and only NBA player to score 100 points in a single game. Chamberlain finished the season with 4,029 points. He remains the only NBA player to score 4,000 points in a single season. He also averaged over 50 points per game. The Warriors moved to San Francisco the following season. Chamberlain returned to Philadelphia in 1965 as a 76er. He led the team to an NBA championship in 1967. Chamberlain won league MVP three times between 1966 and 1968. In 1968, he was traded to the Los Angeles Lakers. He helped the Lakers win the 1972 NBA title and was named the Finals MVP. Chamberlain retired in 1973 as the NBA's top career scorer. He still holds many impressive records. These include most successful shot attempts without a miss with 18 shots, most minutes per game played in a season at 48.5, and most rebounds in a single game with 55.

PROFILE

HEIGHT 7 FT 1 IN

BIRTHDAY AUGUST 21, 1936

POSITION CENTER

YEAR DRAFTED 1959

YEARS ACTIVE 1959–1973

TEAMS
PHILADELPHIA/ SAN FRANCISCO WARRIORS
PHILADELPHIA 76ERS
LOS ANGELES LAKERS

AWARDS & RECORDS

30.1 AVERAGE POINTS

31,419 CAREER POINTS

4.4 AVERAGE ASSISTS

1,045 CAREER GAMES

22.9 AVERAGE REBOUNDS

1979 ELECTED TO BASKETBALL HALL OF FAME

4 TIME MVP

Kareem Abdul-Jabbar played in the NBA for 20 seasons. A dominant center, he held the league's top scoring record for nearly 39 years. His signature **skyhook** helped defeat many great teams.

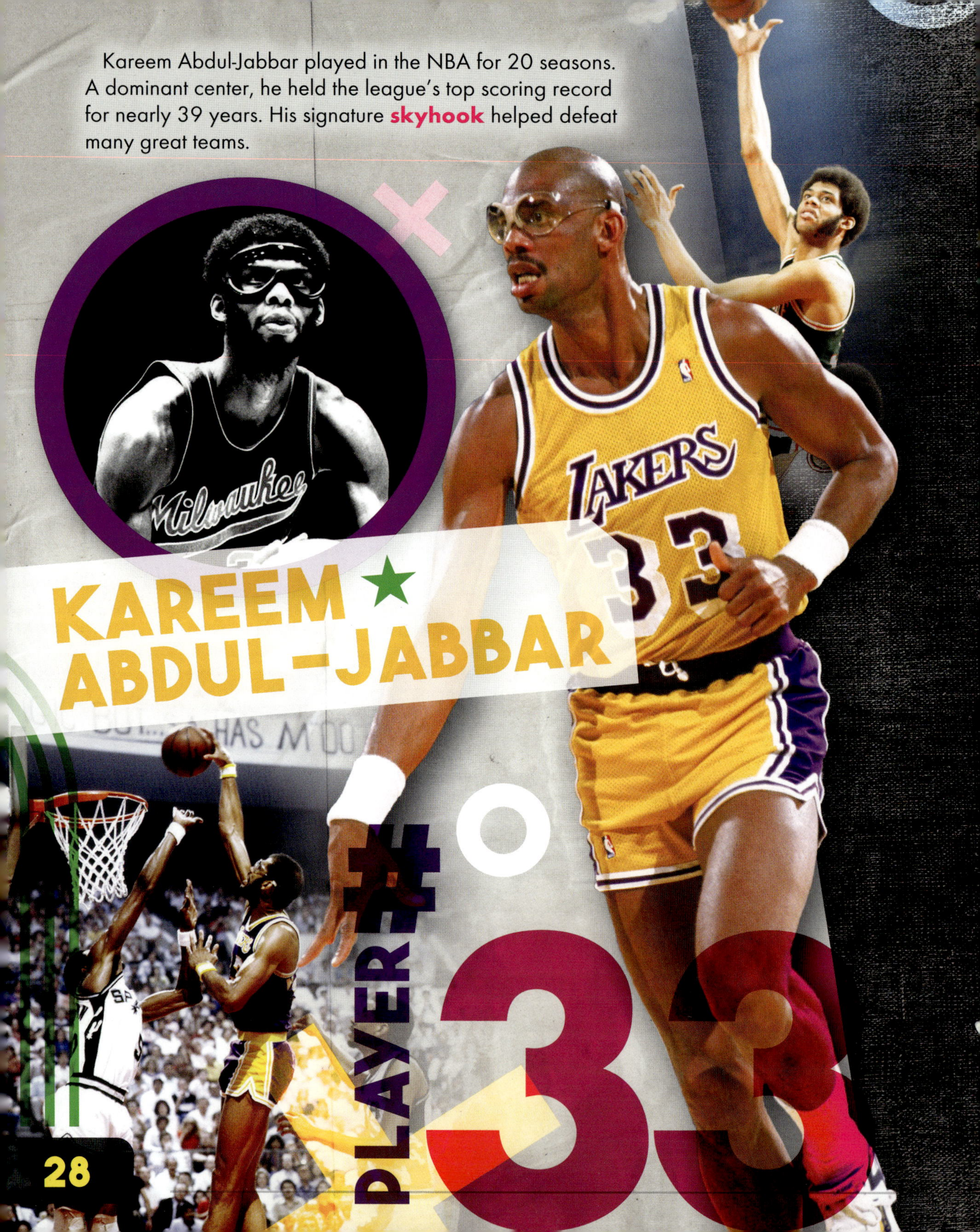

The Milwaukee Bucks drafted Abdul-Jabbar before the 1969–70 season. He was named the Rookie of the Year in his first season. The following season, Abdul-Jabbar led the league in scoring and helped the Bucks sweep the Baltimore Bullets to win their first NBA championship. He also won his first of six league MVP awards.

In 1975, Abdul-Jabbar was traded to the Los Angeles Lakers. He played there for the next 14 seasons. In the 1979–80 season, point guard Magic Johnson joined the team. Together, Abdul-Jabbar and Johnson led the Lakers to five league titles in 1980, 1982, 1985, 1987, and 1988. He retired in 1989 with the longest NBA career up until that point. Abdul-Jabbar was the first NBA player to play 20 seasons. He also holds the records for most MVP awards won.

SKYHOOK

PROFILE

HEIGHT 7 FT 2 IN

BIRTHDAY APRIL 16, 1947

POSITION CENTER

YEAR DRAFTED 1969

YEARS ACTIVE 1969–1989

TEAMS MILWAUKEE BUCKS

LOS ANGELES LAKERS

AWARDS & RECORDS

24.6 AVERAGE POINTS

38,387 CAREER POINTS

3.6 AVERAGE ASSISTS

1,560 CAREER GAMES

11.2 AVERAGE REBOUNDS

1995 ELECTED TO BASKETBALL HALL OF FAME

6 TIME MVP

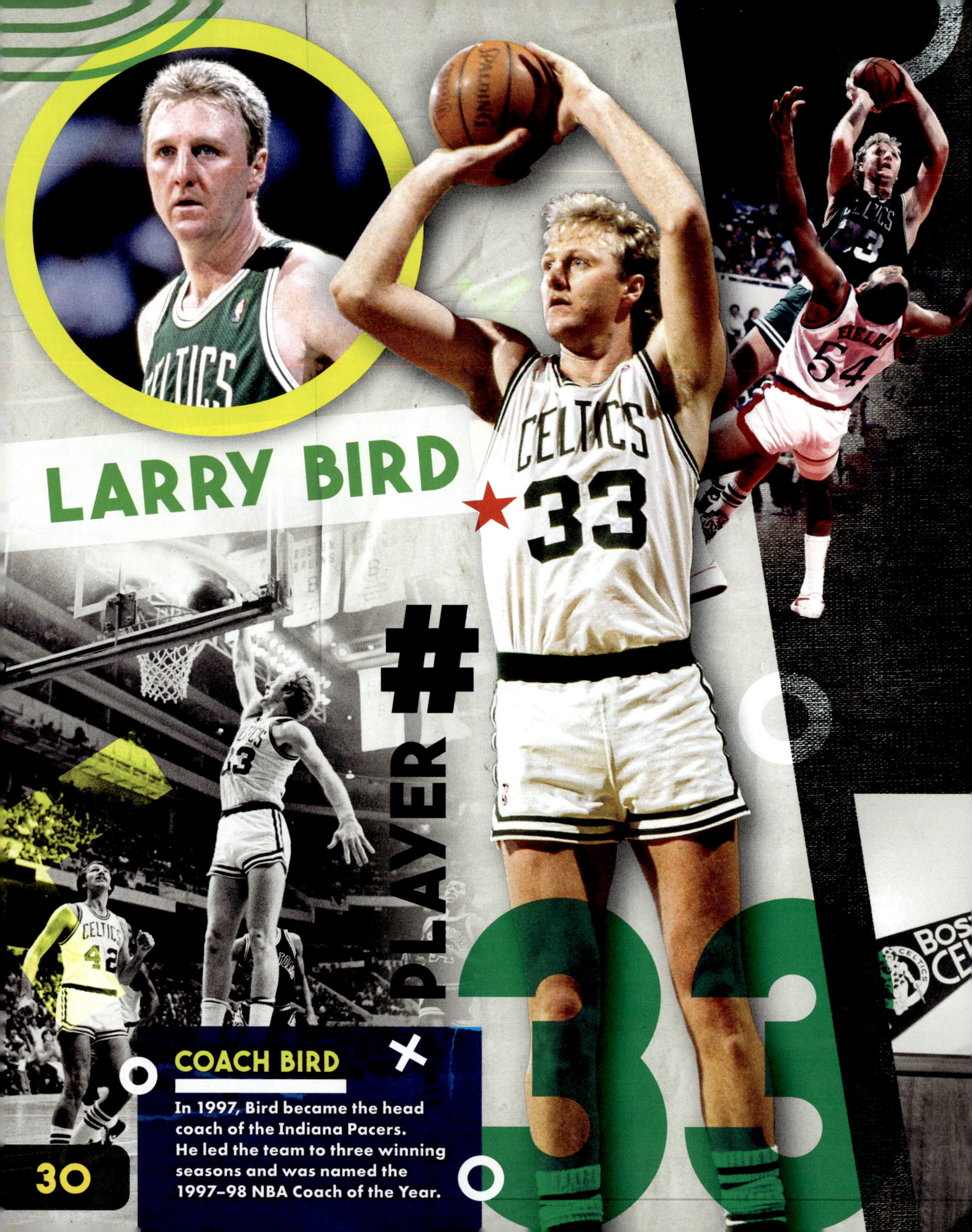

COACH BIRD

In 1997, Bird became the head coach of the Indiana Pacers. He led the team to three winning seasons and was named the 1997–98 NBA Coach of the Year.

Larry Bird played forward for the Boston Celtics for 13 seasons. He was a dependable scorer, passer, rebounder, defender, and **clutch** shooter. Bird played for the Indiana State Sycamores in college, leading the team to an undefeated regular season his senior year. His intense college rivalry with Magic Johnson carried over into the NBA once both players joined the league in 1979. The two would play against each other in three NBA Finals.

Bird immediately made a difference on the Celtics. His 21.3 points per game and 10.4 rebounds per game lifted the Celtics to the top of their division and earned Bird the Rookie of the Year award. With Bird, the Celtics reached the playoffs every season. They won NBA titles in 1981, 1984, and 1986. Bird became the first non-center to win three consecutive MVP awards after winning from 1984 to 1986. Over his career, he was a 12-time All-Star, and he was named All-Star MVP in 1982. He became a fan favorite for his last-second plays to win games. Back problems forced him to retire in 1992. He netted 27,791 career points, averaged 24.3 points per game, and pulled down 8,974 rebounds.

PROFILE

HEIGHT 6 FT 9 IN

BIRTHDAY DECEMBER 7, 1956

POSITION FORWARD

YEAR DRAFTED 1978

YEARS ACTIVE 1979–1992

TEAM BOSTON CELTICS

AWARDS & RECORDS

24.3 AVERAGE POINTS

21,791 CAREER POINTS

6.3 AVERAGE ASSISTS

897 CAREER GAMES

10.0 AVERAGE REBOUNDS

1998 ELECTED TO BASKETBALL HALL OF FAME

3 TIME MVP

MAGIC ★ JOHNSON
PLAYER #32
GRANT
54
LAKERS
32

Earvin "Magic" Johnson spent his 13-year NBA career with the Los Angeles Lakers. He was known for his dramatic passing ability, holding the record for most average assists per game to this day. Johnson was a basketball legend in Michigan before even joining the NBA. A local sportswriter gave him the nickname Magic after watching him play in high school. He was drafted first overall by the Lakers in 1979.

Johnson led the Lakers' "Showtime" offense alongside Kareem Abdul-Jabbar. He helped the Lakers win the NBA Finals. He won the Finals MVP Award for his outstanding performance. In 1982, the Lakers won another championship title. Johnson earned his second Finals MVP. In the 1984 Finals, Johnson met his rival Larry Bird and the Celtics. The Celtics beat the Lakers in seven games. But the Lakers faced the Celtics again in the 1985 and 1987 Finals, defeating them both times. Johnson won Finals MVP for the third time in 1987. He also won league MVP three times between 1987 and 1990. Johnson retired from the NBA in 1991. He made a brief comeback for part of the 1995–96 season. At his final retirement, Johnson held the league record for most assists at 10,141.

PROFILE

HEIGHT 6 FT 9 IN

BIRTHDAY AUGUST 14, 1959

POSITION POINT GUARD

YEAR DRAFTED 1979

YEARS ACTIVE 1979–1991, 1996

TEAM LOS ANGELES LAKERS

AWARDS & RECORDS

- 19.5 AVERAGE POINTS
- 17,707 CAREER POINTS
- 11.2 AVERAGE ASSISTS
- 906 CAREER GAMES
- 7.2 AVERAGE REBOUNDS
- 2002 ELECTED TO BASKETBALL HALL OF FAME
- 3 TIME MVP

Many people consider Michael Jordan to be the greatest basketball players of all time. He earned the nickname "Air Jordan" because of his extraordinary jumping abilities.

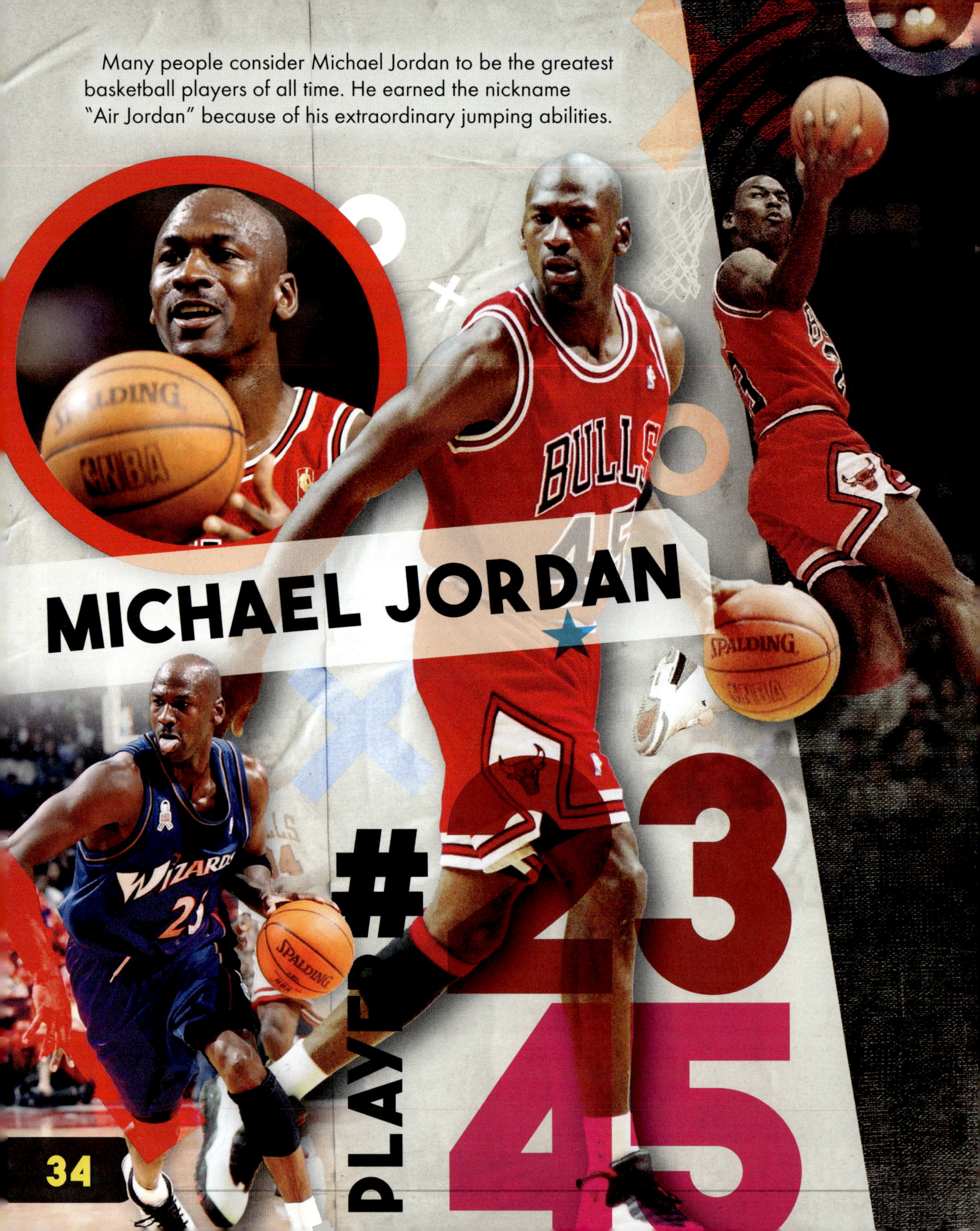

In 1984, Jordan was drafted by the Chicago Bulls. He averaged 28.2 points per game his first season, earning him NBA Rookie of the Year. Jordan led the Bulls to three straight NBA Finals victories from 1991 to 1993. He was named Finals MVP all three times.

In 1993, Jordan took a year away from basketball to play minor league baseball. But he came back to play for the Bulls in 1995. He led the team to a record-setting 72 regular season wins and an NBA Finals victory over the Seattle SuperSonics. The Bulls took back-to-back championship wins, beating the Utah Jazz in 1997. The following year, they met the Jazz in the Finals again. They won in Game 6, with Jordan hitting the final shot to give the Bulls their third straight championship. It was his sixth and final NBA title. Jordan retired after the 1997–98 season. He returned in 2001 to play two more seasons with the Washington Wizards before retiring for good at age 40. He holds the NBA record for the highest career scoring average with 30.1 points per game, Finals MVP wins with six, and most NBA scoring titles with 10.

NEW NUMBER

In 1990, Michael Jordan wore the number 12 for one game. His jersey had been stolen. He did not have a backup, and no one in the stands had a number 23 jersey his size.

PROFILE

HEIGHT 6 FT 6 IN

BIRTHDAY FEBRUARY 7, 1963

POSITION GUARD

YEAR DRAFTED 1984

YEARS ACTIVE 1984–1993, 1995–1998, 2001–2003

TEAMS CHICAGO BULLS, WASHINGTON WIZARDS

AWARDS & RECORDS

30.1 AVERAGE POINTS

32,292 CAREER POINTS

5.3 AVERAGE ASSISTS

1,072 CAREER GAMES

6.2 AVERAGE REBOUNDS

2009 ELECTED TO BASKETBALL HALL OF FAME

5 TIME MVP

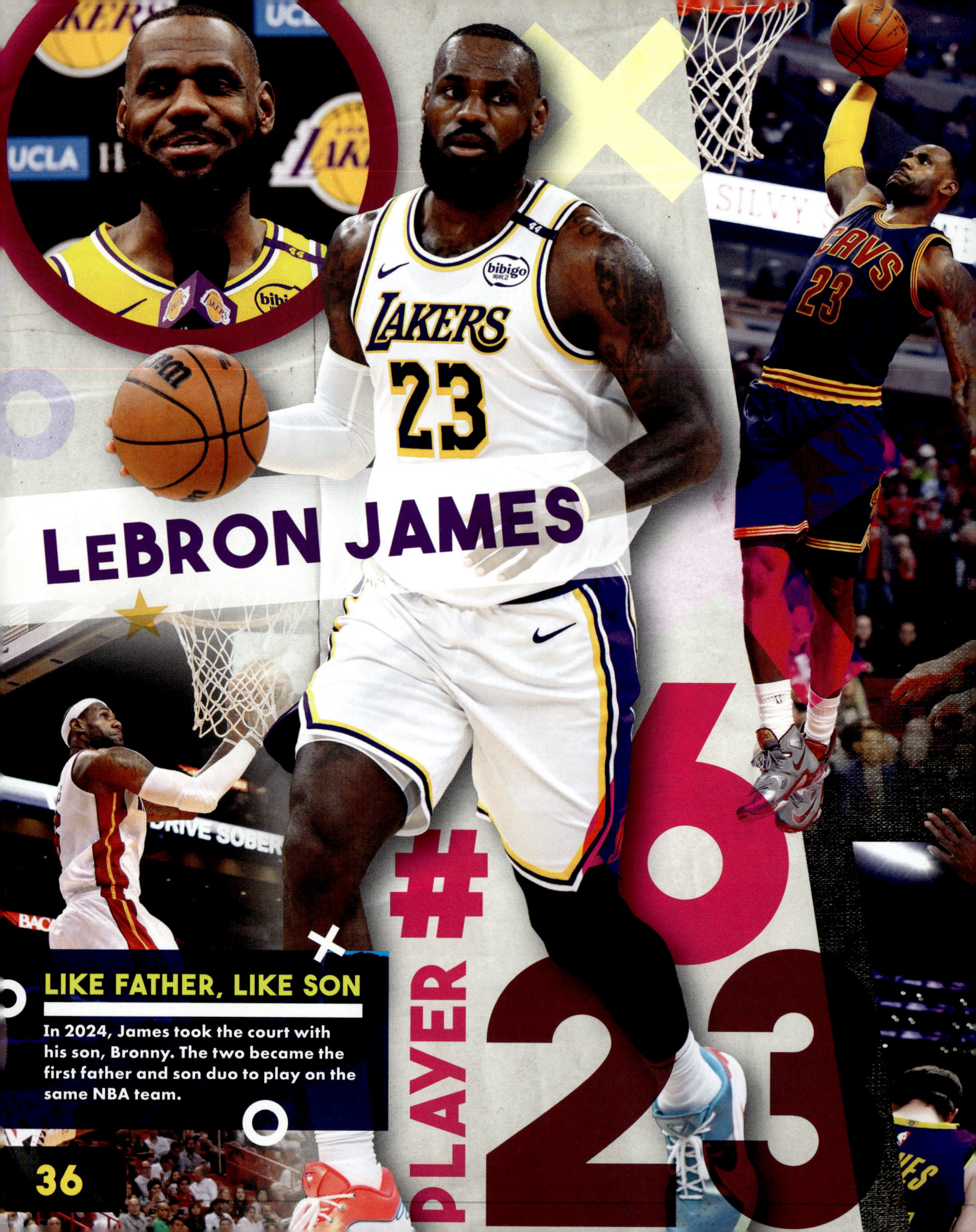

LeBRON JAMES

PLAYER #23

LIKE FATHER, LIKE SON

In 2024, James took the court with his son, Bronny. The two became the first father and son duo to play on the same NBA team.

Some people argue that LeBron James is the best player of all time. In 2003, James was the first overall draft pick by the Cleveland Cavaliers. James led the team in points, steals, and minutes played, earning the Rookie of the Year Award. During the 2007–08 season, James led the league in scoring. He received his first league MVP award after the 2008–09 season. The following season, he averaged 29.7 points per game and was voted MVP for a second time.

James joined the Miami Heat in 2010. This began a streak of James playing in eight Finals in a row from 2011–2018. James led the Heat to back-to-back Finals victories in 2012 and 2013, winning league MVP and Finals MVP each season. He returned to Cleveland before the 2014–15 season. The following season, James helped the Cavaliers win their first title in franchise history. In 2018, James signed with the Los Angeles Lakers. The following season, James helped the Lakers win the Finals to secure his fourth NBA championship and fourth Finals MVP Award. In 2023, James made history by breaking Kareem Abdul-Jabbar's all-time scoring record. In 2024, he scored his 40,000th point and remains the NBA's all-time leading scorer.

PROFILE

HEIGHT 6 FT 9 IN

BIRTHDAY DECEMBER 30, 1984

POSITION FORWARD

YEAR DRAFTED 2003

YEARS ACTIVE 2003–PRESENT

TEAMS CLEVELAND CAVALIERS, MIAMI HEAT, LOS ANGELES LAKERS

AWARDS & RECORDS

AS OF 2025

- 27.0 AVERAGE POINTS
- 42,184 CAREER POINTS
- 7.4 AVERAGE ASSISTS
- 1,562 CAREER GAMES
- 7.5 AVERAGE REBOUNDS
- 4 TIME MVP

MEMORABLE MOMENTS

WILT CHAMBERLAIN'S 100-POINT GAME

On March 2, 1962, Wilt Chamberlain set one of the greatest records in sports history. On this date, Chamberlain and the Philadelphia Warriors faced off against the New York Knicks. By halftime, the Warriors led 79–68, with Chamberlain scoring 41 points. Early into the second half, Chamberlain surpassed 50 points. His teammates began feeding him the ball to see how many points he could score.

With 8 minutes remaining, Chamberlain needed 25 points to reach 100. His teammates gave up easy shots in order to get the ball to him. With 7:51 left in the game, Chamberlain reached 79 points, breaking his personal record. The Knicks tried to stop him. They fouled other Warriors just to keep the ball out of Chamberlain's hands. Chamberlain had 90 points with less than 3 minutes to go. With just over 1 minute remaining, he dunked hard to reach 98. With 46 seconds remaining, Chamberlain's teammate had an easy layup. But instead of taking the shot, he lobbed the ball to Chamberlain, who hit a short shot to hit triple digits! Fans flooded the court to celebrate Chamberlain's 100 points. No other player has come close to breaking this record.

FANS GREET CHAMBERLAIN

CHAMBERLAIN'S 100TH POINT

THE SHOT

CRAIG EHLO'S LAYUP

In the 1989 NBA Playoffs, the Chicago Bulls faced off against the Cleveland Cavaliers in the First Round. The best-of-five series was tied 2–2. The Bulls needed to win Game 5 to advance. It was a tight game throughout, with six lead changes in the final minute of the game. With 6 seconds left on the clock, Michael Jordan sunk a jumper to give the Bulls a 99–98 lead. Cavaliers' guard Craig Ehlo answered with a driving layup to take back the lead. The Cavaliers were up 100–99 with 3 seconds left. The Bulls called a timeout. Coach Doug Collins had one instruction for the team. Get the ball to Jordan.

DOUG COLLINS

Bulls forward Brad Sellers held the inbound pass. But Jordan was double-teamed. Jordan moved right, then made a quick cut left to get open. Sellers passed to Jordan. Jordan grabbed the ball and moved toward the basket. He took a jump shot over Ehlo at the foul line. The ball dropped through the rim at the buzzer, giving the Bulls a last-second 101–100 victory! Jordan leaped into the air with a wild fist pump in celebration.

"The Shot" was the first **buzzer-beater** in a winner-take-all playoff game. It remains one of the greatest clutch moments in NBA history.

JORDAN CELEBRATES

KAWHI LEONARD'S 4-BOUNCE BUZZER-BEATER

In the 2019 Eastern Conference Semifinals, the Toronto Raptors met the Philadelphia 76ers. With the series tied 3–3, it all came down to Game 7. The game was tied at 85 points with less than 2 minutes on the clock. Raptors small forward Kawhi Leonard hit a long 2-point shot to take the lead with 1:41 to go. On the next **possession**, a steal led to another Raptors score, giving Toronto an 89–85 lead. But after two fouls, the 76ers made it a one-point game off of free throws.

With 10 seconds to play, Leonard was fouled. He made one of two free throws to give the Raptors a 90–88 lead. But 76ers forward Jimmy Butler answered with a game-tying layup, leaving 4.2 seconds on the clock. Leonard took the inbound pass. He dribbled to the right corner of the court. Just as time ran out, he took a **fadeaway** shot over the fingertips of defender Joel Embiid. The ball bounced off the rim four times before dropping in, giving the Raptors a last-second 92–90 victory. Leonard's game-winning basket sent Toronto to the Eastern Conference Finals, where they beat the Milwaukee Bucks. The Raptors went on to defeat the Golden State Warriors in the Finals for their first title in franchise history.

FIRST TIME

Kawhi Leonard's game-winning shot was the first game-winning buzzer-beater in a playoff Game 7.

THE NBA BY THE NUMBERS

THE NBA WAS FOUNDED IN 1946 AS THE BAA. THE FIRST NBA GAME WAS PLAYED ON NOVEMBER 1, 1946.

42,184 POINTS

MOST CAREER POINTS

AS OF 2025

LeBRON JAMES

23

PLAYER WITH THE MOST NBA CHAMPIONSHIPS

BILL RUSSELL

11 CHAMPIONSHIPS

GOLDEN STATE WARRIORS

MOST GAMES WON IN A SEASON

AS OF 2025

73 WINS

FOUNDED 1923
OLDEST TEAM
SACRAMENTO KINGS
STEPHEN CURRY
MOST CAREER 3-POINTERS
AS OF 2025
4,058
3-POINTERS
MOST CAREER REBOUNDS
23,924
REBOUNDS
WILT CHAMBERLAIN
LARGEST STADIUM
UNITED CENTER,
CHICAGO BULLS,
CHICAGO, ILLINOIS
20,917
CAPACITY
MOST NBA TITLES
AS OF 2025
BOSTON CELTICS
18
TITLES
MOST CAREER ASSISTS
15,806
ASSISTS
JOHN STOCKTON

GLOSSARY

All-Star Break—a break in the season for the All-Star Game; the All-Star Game is a game between two teams made up of the best players in a league.

bench player—a player on a sports team who comes into the game as a substitute for a starting player

buzzer-beater—a shot made as time ends

clutch—related to incredible skill under pressure with performance that often changes the outcome of the game

commissioner—a person in charge of a sports league

conference—a grouping of teams that often compete against each other

consecutive—one right after the other

dissolved—brought to an end

divisions—groups of teams that often play each other

draft—a process where professional teams choose high school and college athletes to play for them

fadeaway—a jump shot taken while jumping backwards away from the basket

fast break—a play where a player with the ball tries to score before the other team can stop them

franchises—businesses that operate professional sports teams in a league

free agent—an athlete who is not signed to a team and can join any team

headquarters—the main office building of an organization

merge—to join together

playoffs—games played after the regular season is over; playoff games determine with teams play in the championship series.

possession—a period of time in which a team controls the ball

postseason—games played after the regular season

rookie—a first-year player

roster—a list of the players on a team

seeds—the rankings of sports teams within their division, conference, or league

shot clock—a clock that shows a countdown of the time a team has to make a shot

skyhook—a high-arching hook shot; a hook shot is a swooping one-handed shot made by extending one arm out and over the head.

standings—team rankings

swept—won a series of games without any losses

tournament—a series of games in which several teams try to win the championship

WRITE ABOUT IT!

- Many people think either Michael Jordan or LeBron James is the best NBA player of all time. Which one do you think is the better player and **why?**

- Which of the NBA's greatest teams do you think is the best and why? **Do you** think they would be the best team in the league today?

- Which moment in the NBA's history do you think is the most important and **why?**

ALSO CHECK OUT

INDEX

The images in this book are reproduced through the courtesy of: ASSOCIATED PRESS/ AP Images, front cover, pp. 1, 2 (Jordan), 3 (James), 4 (Fun Fact), 5 (all), 6, 7, 8 (all), 9 (all), 10 (all), 12, 13 (bottom), 14 (top, middle), 17 (1946, 1979, 2019), 18, 19, 20 (all), 22 (Bryant), 23, 24 (all), 25 (Curry), 27, 30 (inset, top), 31, 34 (Jordan, right), 36 (James, top), 38, 39 (all), 42 (middle, bottom), 43, 44 (James), 45 (Chamberlain); bill Belknap/ Alamy Stock Photo, front cover, p. 1; Anastasiarasputin/ Wikimedia Commons, front cover, p. 1; RO9A3387/ Wikimedia Commons, front cover, p. 1; lev radin, front cover, p. 1; ZUMA Press, Inc./ Alamy Stock Photo, pp. 3 (Bird), 19 (Bird), 21 (Jordan), 22 (Fisher), 30 (Bird), 34 (bottom), 35; MediaNews Group/ Bay Area News via Getty Images/ Getty Images, p. 4; AfriPics.com/ Alamy Stock Photo, p. 6 (headquarters); Sarah Stier/ Getty Images, p. 11 (draft); Staff Sgt. Crystal Housman/ Wikimedia Commons, pp. 11 (trophy), 45 (trophy); Sasha Haas/ Flickr, p. 12 (shot clock); Bettmann/ Getty Images, pp. 13 (top), 26 (top); Focus On Sport/ Getty Images, pp. 14 (bottom), 15, 28 (top), 45 (Stockton); Sporting News Archive/ Getty Images, p. 15 (inset); John Biever/ Getty Images, p. 16 (inset); Julien Bacot/ BAL/ Getty Images, p. 16; ABA/ Wikimedia Commons, p. 17 (1967); Nikeush/ Wikimedia Commons, p. 17 (1984); PCN Photography/ Alamy Stock Photo, pp. 21 (inset), 32 (inset, main), 46 (main); Ezra Shaw/ Getty Images, p. 25 (Durant); Paul Vathis/ Wikimedia Commons, pp. 26 (100), 39 (100); Fred Palumbo/ Wikimedia Commons, p. 26 (bottom); RLFE Pix/ Alamy Stock Photo, pp. 26 (main), 48 (main); The Sporting News Archives/ Wikimedia Commons, p. 28 (inset); Peter Read Miller/ Getty Images, p. 28 (bottom); Stephen Dunn/ Getty Images, p. 28 (main); Charlie Kloppenburg/ Alamy Stock Photo, p. 29; Boston Globe/ Getty Images, p. 30 (bottom); Rick Stewart/ Getty Images, p. 32 (left); Carl Skalak/ Getty Images, pp. 33, 40 (all), 41 (inset); Steve Lipofsky Basketballphoto.com/ Wikimedia Commons, p. 34 (inset); dpa picture alliance/ Alamy Stock Photo, p. 36 (inset); Tribune Content Agency LLC/ Alamy Stock Photo, p. 36 (bottom); Luke Hales/ Getty Images, p. 37; Chicago Tribune/ Getty Images, p. 41; Vaughn Ridley/ Getty Images, p. 42 (top); Unknown/ Wikimedia Commons, p. 44 (Russell); Sam Hodde/ Getty Images, p. 45 (Curry); Wirestock Creators, p. 45 (Stadium); Px Images/ Alamy Stock Photo, p. 45 (background).